Once upon a time...

To: Baby Campbell

From: Priya Thakore

And they lived happily ever after.

A message for children of all ages
and the child in every adult.

"Each soul comes to the Earth with gifts."

Gary Zukav, *The Seat of the Soul*

The Twelve Gifts of Birth

By Charlene Costanzo
Photography by Jill Reger
Illustration by Wendy Wassink Ackison

HarperResource

An Imprint of HarperCollinsPublishers

HarperCollins books may be purchased for educational, business, or sales promotional use.
For information, please write to: Special Markets Department, HarperCollins Publishers Inc.,
10 East 53rd Street, New York, New York 10022.

Photography Copyright © 2001 by Jill Reger
Photography Direction by Tina Higgins
Illustraton Copyright © 2001 by Wendy Wassink Ackison
Book Design by Karen C. Heard

A previous edition of this book was published in 1999 by *Featherfew*™.
Printed in Japan by Toppan Printing Co., Ltd.
FIRST HARPER EDITION PUBLISHED 2001

Library of Congress Cataloging-in-Publication has been applied for.

ISBN 0-06-621104-2

01 02 03 04 05 10 9 7 6 5 4 3

For Stephanie and Krista
and You

"Royal dignity was yours from the day you were born."

 Psalms 110:3

"Every human person is noble and of royal blood."

Meister Eckhart

❧

This book belongs to:

_____

Presented with love by:

_____

On this day:

_____

With these thoughts:

_____

_____

_____

_____

Once upon a time, a long time ago,
when princes and princesses lived in faraway
kingdoms, royal children were given twelve
special gifts when they were born. You may have
heard the stories. Twelve wise women of the kingdom, or fairy
godmothers as they were often called, traveled swiftly to the castle
whenever a new prince or princess came into the world.
Each fairy godmother pronounced a noble gift upon the royal baby.

As time went on, the wise women came to understand that the
twelve royal gifts of birth belong to every child, born anywhere,
at anytime. They yearned to proclaim the gifts to all children,
but the customs of the land did not allow that.

One day when the wise women gathered
together they made this prophecy:

Some day all the children of the

world will learn the truth about

their noble inheritance. When that

happens a miracle will unfold on

the kingdom of Earth.

Some day is near.

Here is the secret they

want you to know.

At the wondrous moment

you were born,

as you took your first breath,

a great celebration was held

in the heavens

and twelve

magnificent gifts

were granted

to you.

The first gift is Strength.

*May you remember to call upon it
whenever you need it.*

The second gift is Beauty.

May your deeds reflect its depth.

The third gift is Courage.

May you speak and act with confidence and use courage to follow your own path.

The fourth gift is Compassion.

May you be gentle with yourself and others. May you forgive those who hurt you and yourself when you make mistakes.

The fifth gift is Hope.

Through each passage and season,
may you trust the goodness of life.

The sixth gift is Joy.

*May it keep your heart open and
filled with light.*

The seventh gift is Talent.

*May you discover
your own special abilities and contribute
them toward a better world.*

The eighth gift is Imagination.

May it nourish your visions and dreams.

The ninth gift is Reverence.

May you appreciate the wonder that you are and the miracle of all creation.

The tenth gift is Wisdom.

Guiding your way, wisdom will lead you through knowledge to understanding. May you hear its soft voice.

The eleventh gift is Love.

It will grow each time you give it away.

The twelfth gift is Faith.

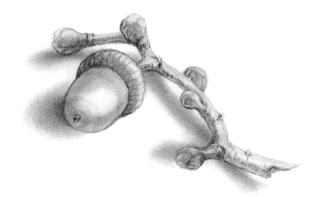

May you believe.

Now you know about your twelve gifts of birth.

But there is more to the secret

that the wise women knew.

Use your gifts well and you will discover others,

among them a gift that is uniquely you.

See these noble gifts in other people.

Share the truth and be ready for the miracle to unfold

as the prophecy of the wise women comes true.

The Twelve Gifts of Birth reminds us to recognize dignity in ourselves and others. When presented to young children, this message can help form within them a strong foundation of self-respect and values. May you build upon that foundation by reinforcing daily their sense of worth. Read to them often, listen to them with your heart and help them see their gifts developing in each day's experience.

To learn more about *The Twelve Gifts of Birth* or to contact Charlene Costanzo, please visit www.thetwelvegiftsofbirth.com

A portion of the author's profits derived from *The Twelve Gifts of Birth* is donated to programs that prevent abuse and promote the well-being of children.